Bil Keane

FAWCETT GOLD MEDAL • NEW YORK

"What's a pigsty?"

"What's 129 divided by 4?"

"Can you help me with this composition, Mommy? It's called 'Learning to Think for Yourself!'"

"Kissing's over."

"When your hands and face feel very cold that's because of the chill factory."

"Daddy, what date does snow begin?"

"Dolly's throwing the broken pieces away
without drying them."

"Hold it, Daddy! You've got me all in one leg!"

"Was his win legit or are you just buttering him up to help rake the leaves?"

"Do we have to start bein' good two weeks before Christmas or three?"

"Now, listen to me. We are NOT buying any toys."

"It won't cost you any money, Mommy. You
could just write a check."

"Why did you put your first and last name on
this card for Mommy and Daddy?
They know Dolly who."

"Dear Santa: I want No. 5815 on page 10."

"Are you sure you can remember all of this without writing it down?"

"Grandma only likes religious cards so I'm sendin' her this one with St. Nick on it."

"We mailed your family a Christmas card today so you better send us one."

"Can you giftwrap something with your eyes closed? It's for you."

"First, I have all the clothes I need."

"Jeffy won't kiss me and I'm standin' here
under the mistletoe."

"Dear Santa, bless Mommy and Daddy and
. . . I mean, Dear God, bless Mommy and..."

"I had Mommy's wrapped at the store, but I did Daddy's myself."

"It'll look a lot happier once it's wearin' all its lights and stuff."

"Oh, dear—the Beasleys sent us one and we
took them off our list."
"We'll send them a New Year's card."

"Who mixed all the burned-out bulbs in with the good ones?"

"Kittycat's ruinin' Christmas!"

"Is it time to hang our stockings by the
chimney with care?"

"It's wrapped in the same kind of paper Santa
used on my present."

"What's a warranty?"

"Those aren't unmentionables, Grandma. They're bra and panties."

"Dolly says my robot is a girl and I wanted a boy robot!"

"I CAN'T go to bed. Mr. Thirkhill's sleeping in it."

"There goes my New Year's revolution."

"I know all the months. This one is Valentine's, this one is Easter, this one's Mother's Day. . . ."

"You lost your mittens? You naughty kitten!
Then you shall have no pie."

"Are these the dogs kids love to bite or the
ones that go 'Oh, I wish I were a
da-dee-da-da wiener...' ?"

"These sandwiches are very small. They must be just samples."

"I keep putting on weight. Does that mean I
hafta go on a diet?"

"When it snows I like to listen to the quiet."

"Do the bumps on a 'B' go toward the living
room or the kitchen?"

". . . and on cold winter mornings the milk bottles would have high hats on them."

"What are milk bottles, Grandma?"

" . . . and they lived happily ever after."
"Ever after what?"

"Dolly Parton has a hairdo, and Joe Garagiola has a hairDON'T."

"You peel two and I'll peel two."

"Oh, they're all fine. What I mean is their health is good."

"When you squeeze it, it yells."

"... and each snowflake is different from any other one. It has six sides and a design of its very own."

"Boy, Dolly! You're not a very good ad for girls."

"That top must be everybody-proof."

"I have an itch and I can't scratch it."

"Yellow is MY favorite color. You'll have to pick a different favorite color."

"Good night! If anybody wants to play with my Uncle Wiggly game, that's OK."

"This is nothing. When I was your age we had snow that came all the way up to here on me."

"Uh-huh . . . yes . . . yes . . . sure . . . uh-huh
. . . right . . . yes . . . certainly . . . yes . . ."
"Must be Grandma."

"Wait a minute, Mommy. I want to see this commercial."

"Watch how Daddy reels it in."

"You're lyin', PJ! I can tell 'cause your nose is starting to grow."

"I just got a spanking. Daddy hurt his hand
and I didn't feel a thing."

"Can you help us with something, Mommy?"

"This thing shut off by itself. How did it know when my hands were dry?"

"I don't think I can play basketball till I grow
up closer to the basket."

"Daddy's shining his shoes with PJ again."

"It's gonna snow tonight. Do I have to do my homework 'cause maybe they'll close the schools tomorrow?"

"That's my little brother's potty train."

"This IS my homework. In history we're studying the fifties.

"That's enough until tomorrow. Are you gonna
pay me when the whole path is shoveled or at
the end of each day?"

"Do you know where I hid the Valentine card I
made for you?"

"Hey, this heart has two floors!"

"It's OK. He landed
butter-side up."

"I know we're not gettin' company. Mommy's
using the tablecloth with a hole in it."

"I didn't do it . . . . My fingers did."

"Beats me why I ain't gettin' no better marks in English."

"Can I connect the dots on your tie?"

"At Grandma's I don't have to sit on a booster chair. She lets me sit on her phone book."

"I don't see why Daddy likes to snore. I tried it
last night and it's hard work!"

"If apples are 15 cents each, how many would you . . .?"
"Aren't apples sold by the pound?"

"It doesn't look like a button to me."

"My shirt doesn't say anything."

"This one's good for the waistline. Drop a
bunch of marbles on the floor . . ."

"If March comes in like a lion it goes out like a light. Right, Mommy?"

"In the first place, kittens don't wear mittens,
and in the second place, they don't like pie."

"The sink has something stuck in its throat."

"Think harder, P.J. I can't hear a thing."

"It's from Mommy — a dish towel."

"Here, Sam!"

"Sugar is real loud when you walk on it."

"You're wrong. I just have a slight case of the flu. I am NOT dying of old age."

"Why do you put that little hat on your finger?"

"Don't worry, Mommy, I didn't walk on your papers."

"One sitter plays games and another one reads to us.
What do you do?"

"Know what, Mommy? There are 25 inches of tooth paste in a tube."

"I'm having trouble figure-outing this puzzle."

"I forgot to tell you — I need an asparagus
costume for the play tomorrow."

"Mommy says fighting doesn't 'complish a thing. You should talk it out."

"Look! That's where they make clouds."

"For 'current events' homework we're s'posed to read the newspaper."

"Mommy, this brush is losin' its whiskers."

"It's one of those old folk dances."

"It's a drink of water for Daddy."
"That's a good boy."

"You better get two boxes. That's the kind
Daddy likes."

"I'm trying out my new boots."

"Eddie's family has a machine that watches
TV for them."

"Mommy sends that little rocket ship to get money."

"You got a D in math."
"WE got a D in math."

"Hi! In case I forget — I had a very nice time and thank you."

"You are not going out, Kittycat, and I'm not
discussing it any further."

"I'm SEVEN, Mommy. Do I still hafta take baby aspirin?"

"I made some words, Mommy. Will you tell me what they are?"

"Did they name you 'Grandma' when you were a baby?"

"Can we wish for something that costs over five dollars?"

"You can call me Billy, or you can call me Will,
or you can call me Willy, or you can call
me Bill, or you can call me B, or you
can call me William — but you
doesn't hafta call me JUNIOR!"

"Rise and shine what?"

"My new shoes look like little police cars."

"...And we have flowers and a table cloth,
Billy got a haircut and the
carpet's vacuumed..."

"This is where you sweep your feet, Grandma."

"You have two pieces of candy and I give you five more . . ."

"Can we have some, too?"

"You don't need a towel, Mommy. The rug
drank the milk up."

"ONE fly?"

"I'm gonna help you, Mommy. When you want
some nuts cracked put them under my
rockin' horse."

"I can name that tune in one note!"

"It sure is muddy out today."

"We have bones all over our insides, don't we?"

"It's just so you can test your furniture polish like they do on TV."

"Hold on a minute, Mother, Billy wants to talk to you . . ."

"Wanna wiggle my loose tooth?"

You can have lots more fun
with
BIL KEANE and
THE FAMILY CIRCUS